Get Selfish

THE WAY IS THROUGH

By Joanna Hunter

ISBN **978-0-9933027-0-1**

First Edition 2015 - **Paperback**

Authored by Joanna Hunter

Cover design by Paul Hunter

Published by My Inner Peace Publishing

Formatted by Esther/Randy Klinger

To the Happiness Seekers from around the world, with my heartfelt hope the search is over – this book is dedicated to you. May we all have the courage to shine our own true light with joy.

Get Selfish
Table of Contents

Seven Steps to creating lasting happiness & abundance in your life!

Believe Nothing,
no matter where you read it
or who has said it, not even
if I have said it, unless it agrees
with your own common sense.

~Buddha

Foreword

Over the course of many years, I have been on a journey of learning how to create happiness in my life. Like many of you, I wanted to be happy, I tried to be happy, I worked at being happy, but it didn't always work out.

At first I thought it was a lack of something: A lack of friends, of money, of fulfilment, of direction, or even a lack of 'Ikea' furniture in my life. So I shopped, I filled my life with what the magazines told me I needed. I worked my socks off, because more money was the solution, right? But nothing filled the void… and I didn't know why.

So there I was, spreading myself so thin that the cracks were starting to appear. My debt was sky high and my house was jam-packed full of stuff that was going to be SO useful one day. I had a ton of plans that were all going to happen as if by magic, right after I was perfect—you know, like thinner, leaner, prettier, younger, smarter, happier, taller... I was miserable, but I had one thought that ran on a loop in my head: "There's got to be more to life."

"There's got to be more to life!" I kept saying it to myself and to the universe in general, until one day, the universe began answering back.

This little book is the book the universe co-wrote with me, and my way of passing on some of those answers to you, with the hope that they will illuminate your life path as they have illuminated mine.

Step One

~WHAT IS GET SELFISH?

The World can
only be Free
When men are content in
Themselves & each draws on
His own Fountain.

~ George William Russell

The Fountain

Before we begin, I want to tell you a little story from my own journey, and share a symbol that came to me in a meditation, which is relevant to everyone. It changed my outlook, on myself and my life, in a dramatic way.

In the course of my own journey towards happiness and fulfilment, I've been to many workshops and met many kinds of teachers.

During one particular workshop, we were guided into a meditation based on an ancient Hawaiian understanding that everything has a soul, and that the soul is the universal source of everything. This includes the quality of abundance. The goal of the meditation was to meet the soul/source of our own personal abundance. "Exciting stuff!" I thought, and went into the meditation filled with anticipation. We were to imagine ourselves in a garden, where, atop a hill, we would come face to face with the soul of our own personal abundance.

The garden I saw in my mind's eye was magnificent. I have never seen such a lush, green place. Soft, springy grass stretched for miles; every tree and bush was overflowing with colourful flowers and golden fruit. Every animal you could ever imagine lived there in perfect harmony. As I moved through this garden, my excitement mounted. I mean, if this was the garden of my abundance, what was my *soul* of abundance going to look like?!

Look within, within us is the fountain of good & it will ever bubble up if thou will ever dig

-Marcus Aurelius

Slowly, I made my way up the hill, savouring the amazing greenery and the other-worldly colours of the flowers and fruit. So, it was no slight shock to find, when I reached the top of the hill, that I was on cracked, dry earth, in front of a stagnant, dirty, three-tiered fountain. Was this the soul and source of my abundance? Surely not?

I looked all around me at the landscape, its natural beauty calling to me, and then reluctantly let my eyes fall back on the fountain; what the hell? How could this be? Even grass didn't grow here! I was pulled from my confused musings by a small, famished-looking boy, dressed only in rags. He was scraping a metal cup through the dirty water at the bottom tier of the fountain. The cup made a terrible noise, as horrific as nails on a chalkboard, as he dragged it along. I called for him to stop, but he took no notice, even as I yelled that he would surely get sick from the dirty water.

As the child disappeared, I thought, "This is terrible, what can I do? How can I make this right?" As if to answer my question, barrier tape—like the police put up to temporarily keep people out—materialised around the fountain. To my amazed surprise, the top tier of the fountain began to fill with water. The first tier spilled the dirty water into the second tier, which in turn spilled it into the third. Eventually, the dirty water overflowed onto the ground. The cracked, dry hill top turned to mud, and before my very eyes, grass began to grow again. The more the water flowed, the clearer it became, until the fountain looked new, the water itself sparkled, and the

"When you do things from your soul, you feel a river moving in you, a joy."

-Rumi

ground around it matched the lush greenery of the rest of the garden. As I looked around, I thought, "Yes, this is more like it!" Finally, this fountain, the soul of my abundance, really matched its surroundings! With that thought, the police barrier-tape disappeared, and a crowd of children, with cups and eager faces, appeared. Instead of scraping their cups, as the first child had done, they simply held them aloft, and the overflow filled them with cool, clear water. There was more than enough for everyone!

I came out of the meditation knowing I'd had a profound (if not slightly trippy) experience, but it wasn't until a couple of weeks later that I finally had my "ah-ha" moment. I realised that I was the fountain. I had almost nothing left to give, and what I *did* have was like the fountain's dirty water; it would surely make someone sick. I was sick-sick and tired.

The water represented my energy. I simply had none left. If I really wanted there to be more to life, if I really wanted to help others from a place of abundance, I was going to have to give to myself first. I was going to have to construct my own police tape around myself, so I would have a chance to fill up again, and have something healthy to give. I was going to have to do what I had always thought of as selfish: I was going to have to put myself first. Not as an act of pure selfishness, but as an expression of love—starting with self-love.

Now, looking back, it seems so logical: How could I truly help others unless I was willing to help myself?

You Can Never Cross The Ocean,
Unless You Have
The Courage
To Lose Sight Of
The Shore.

-Christopher Columbus

It's like putting your own oxygen mask on before helping others with theirs. If I worked on filling myself up, nurturing myself, I could become that source of never-ending abundant energy that has more than enough to give, and flows forever.

So that was my first step: I decided to Get Selfish! But all by itself, that doesn't get you very far. Instead, it raised an essential question: What did I need to be nourished?

The answer obviously didn't lie in the "stuff" I filled my life with. Oh no, my life was full of stuff, but I was still filled with lack. I was like the famished boy scraping the bottom of the dirty fountain, and I constantly looked to things and other people to fill that void inside me. But how could they? In all of us, both the void and the fountain are within. Only we can connect with our own source, only we *ourselves* can tell when the void is full; others can guide us, true, but only we can find our own answers.

It was suddenly very clear to me that the only place to go for answers was to that one place I had never fully looked: Inside of myself. I was going to have to go through all the layers of conditioning, illusion, and defence, all the faulty thinking and false values, to find what is true for me and what nourishes me.

I called this step *"going through"*. It has since become my understanding that we don't grow in life, or get what we want, by going around the things that block us. It's an illusion that there is a way around our blocks in the first place, and that can keep us stuck.

15

THE Soul ALWAYS KNOWS
WHAT TO DO TO HEAL ITSELF,
THE CHALLENGE IS
TO SILENCE THE MIND.

—ANON

Our challenges have lots of answers for us. We need to face what is blocking us honestly, with compassion for ourselves, and go through whatever process is needed for us to deepen as people and become happier.

I now follow these two steps in my own life and unashamedly call this process:

Get Selfish! The way is through.

It is important when pursuing our own self interest, we should be 'Wise Selfish' and not 'Foolish Selfish'.

Being Foolish Selfish means pursuing our own interests in a narrow, short sighted way.

Being Wise Selfish means taking a broader view and recognising that our own long term individual interest lies in the welfare of everyone.

Being Wise Selfish means being compassionate.

– Dalai Lama

Getting Selfish

Getting selfish, for me, is about a thousand loving actions towards myself. At its basic level, it is self-care, and the strength to finally say, "I am good enough – I am worthy." It is honouring myself and valuing myself, listening and responding to my own needs. Thus, I become a person I love to be.

Do you like nurturing listeners, people who are respectful and considerate? I know I do! Getting selfish is about doing what we do for others, but doing it for ourselves, and by the very action of lovingly taking care of ourselves, we become more loving and considerate people to everyone. If we love ourselves, it becomes much easier to accept love from others, and when we ourselves are nourished, we have more love to give to others. The best part is that we can do it for ourselves by just listening to ourselves! There's no need to wait for a saviour of any kind.

Have you ever felt guilty saying no to someone just because you are plain worn out, or just not that into their shenanigans anymore? Instead of resting, because you really have no energy left, you tell yourself you *should* have helped that person, and the guilt eats you up; so you now feel you are a "baddie", as well as being tired. It's a no-win situation for everyone involved.

If people don't take you seriously, or consider your feelings and needs, it is possible that it's because you don't either?

I Have
Chosen to be

HAPPY

Because it is good for
My health

-Voltaire

The guilt you feel for not helping the other person comes from not valuing yourself as much as you value that other person. Were you not tired? Who decided that the other person's needs were worth more than yours? Are we not all equals? Why should we feel guilty for listening to ourselves and responding to that input?

I want you to remember that you are a person too. Only **you** can make yourself matter. Who made other people's needs more important than yours? I am going to get in your face here and say, quite bluntly, "You did!"

By that very unconscious action of not honouring ourselves or our primary relationship—which is with ourselves—all other relationships in your life are also held to this standard, and reflect the value we give ourselves, because the outside world is always only a reflection of our inner one. Then, we get angry or feel let down when others don't respect us or consider our needs. So we complain, and grumble to ourselves and others, and since complaining is a negative energy, things keep going downhill. It's easy to see why we can have such trouble loving ourselves, or even considering ourselves worthy, when we *ourselves* have judged complainers as annoying or even horrible people.

The guilt stems from a lack inside us which is a manifestation of fear—mainly the fear of not being good enough. This guilt is actually the universe helping us by highlighting that something is not right. Anytime we feel bad, the universe is helping us by showing us that our energy is not all it could be in that moment.

I am mine,
Before I am ever,
Anyone else's.

-Nayyirah Waheed

The universe is presenting us with a choice at a deep inner level: *Empowered*, or *powerless*? What will you choose to be?

Each time we put other people's needs before our own, or feel guilty when we attend to our own needs, we are sending a message to the universe. The message says, "I am not worthy of being listened to or of having my needs met." The universe responds accordingly, because you've just told it that you are not worth taking care of. As a result, we don't get what we need, and we operate from a base of nearly empty, which, in turn, creates more lack in our lives.

I want to ask you another question: Who can you help when you are at empty? Who can you help when you feel so downtrodden that even the thought of getting out of bed is too much?

You see, the world is not served by your piling more and more onto yourself until you break. If you do that, you become just one more casualty, instead of being a helper. The world is served by your getting selfish, filling your own vessel up first, connecting to your own inner energy of abundance. Only from a place of being nourished and in-touch with your own personal abundance can you give and give and give. Giving will only ever feel joyous if it comes from an empowered state of being—from a state of connection to your own source with love. And to connect with love, to become an expression of love, you have to first love yourself.

WE CANNOT OUTPERFORM OUR LEVEL OF SELF-ESTEEM. WE CANNOT DRAW TO OURSELVES MORE THAN WE THINK WE ARE WORTH.

~IYANLA VANZANT

This will reconnect you with your true nature, which is love and abundance. Now, this energy can fill your entire being, and you will shine like a beautiful beacon for yourself and the world to see.

As we let our light shine,
we unconsciously give
other people permission
to do the same

-Marianne Williamson

The Simple Truth

Getting selfish begins obviously with your*self*. So, before you can get to the good stuff, and have your fountain 'runneth over' and all that jazz, you are going to have to deal with yourself. More importantly, give to yourself.

However, the hard truth is we have become so proficient at lying to ourselves that most of us don't even know we are doing it anymore. We need to begin to take our heads out of the sand and, in effect, stop the lies.

Now, you might be wondering, if you can't tell you are lying to yourself, how will you know what is a lie and what is the truth?

First, we have to understand the truth of what we are;

We don't **have** a soul—yes, it's true—we **have** a body. **We are** **the soul**.

There's a real difference in believing we *are* a body and *have* a soul, as opposed to the truth, which is that we *are* the soul and we *have* a body.

The simple truth is our bodies, in the grand scheme of things, are temporary. They are the most amazing things we'll ever own, but are still just temporary vessels—they won't be 'us' forever. Our minds are also incredible bits of kit, but they are subject to filters and belong to the body, so they are also temporary in the grand scheme of things.

YOU DON'T HAVE A SOUL,
YOU ARE A SOUL.
YOU HAVE A BODY.

-C.S LEWIS

Our truth lies with our souls, which are pure energy and immortal. They live forever, because energy cannot be destroyed. One of the laws of physics states:

Energy cannot be created, nor can it be destroyed, it can only change form.

When the human body dies, energy is released, and that energy is our soul. We *are* our souls. What is more, our souls are hard-wired for happiness and abundance! We know this, because happiness feels good, and negative 'stuff' feels bad; even as children we are aware of this.

Since this is a universe entirely comprised of energy, our souls are what link us to that abundant source of energy. That is the birth place of our abundance and happiness. It is the nature of our souls to be happy and abundant, for our souls are connected to the source, and the nature of that source is LOVE.

What's more, the soul never lies! We just have to learn to speak its language.

Step Two

~CREATE THE SPACE FOR HEALING

"Above all else to thy own self be true..."

~ William Shakespeare

Bathtub of Life

We need to extend the 'barrier-tape' around us first, to create a space within us in which we can grow and nurture ourselves. That means you are going to have to get comfortable with, what for many, is an uncomfortable word: The word 'no'.

This is not randomly saying 'no', it is saying 'no' when everything inside you says it, too. It's giving yourself permission to listen to yourself, be true to yourself, and heal your primary relationship, which is *with* yourself. It's like finally saying 'yes' to you!

The universe is perfect, and in saying "no", we open up new avenues for more positive energy to be exchanged. Saying "no" all the time isn't a forever thing, and by looking after number one, there will come a time when we will begin to overflow with happiness. It's about filling our own vessel first. Putting our own oxygen mask on before we help others wear theirs.

Think of your body as a bathtub with the taps always on (that's the universe endlessly giving), but if the plug of the bath is out, then the bath never has a chance to really fill. Being true to yourself is like plugging your own bath. The bath can finally fill, and like any vessel, it can only take so much filling. There must come a point where it overflows. It's the same with us: If we plug our energy leaks, the things we do that drain us, then it is inevitable that we will fill up with energy and overflow.

Self-care is not selfish.
You cannot serve from
an empty vessel!

– Eleanor Brownn

If we give of our overflow, there will always be enough energy for ourselves and for anyone else we want to help, as we will be operating from the energy of abundance. Remember, the taps are always on, the universe is always giving; we are always being filled. So, it's simply a matter of whether the plug is in or out.

If we give to ourselves first, we will be full, and never self-pitying or envious of others, because there will be no reason to be; being true to ourselves plugs the lack.

Align yourself to the *truth* of you, in order to step into the *power* of you. By being true to yourself, you become the person that deserves all good things in your own mind. Considering that your thoughts create your reality by attracting in "like" energy, becoming a person who deserves all good things in your own mind is vital to achieving happiness, fulfilment, and the life you want.

This is an essential step in creating a better reality for yourself—to extend love and compassion for your *own* SELF first. It's only by allowing love in for ourselves that we can finally fill up with it, and from there, real love and compassion can flow to others.

This will become the foundation on which you build your solid, unlimited Life.

TO MAKE THE
RIGHT CHOICES IN
LIFE YOU HAVE
TO GET IN
TOUCH WITH
YOUR SOUL

-ˢDEEPAK CHOPRA

Now here's a choice for you...

Do you want to live in an infinitely abundant universe?

Or

Do you want to live in a universe with a "lack of", where there is never enough?

The choice is yours.

No, I am not crazy!!! It truly is *your* choice. This is what is meant by free will. We have a daily, second-by-second, choice of how we perceive the world around us. In life, we have victims and winners, but there is no difference between the two, other than the reality the individuals have **chosen** to inhabit.

One choice speaks of self-love; the other of unworthiness. One choice is made from a position of being full of self-love; the other of lack. It's up to each of us to have a loving and nurturing relationship with ourselves, so we can become full to overflowing. This is how we benefit ourselves and the world as a whole.

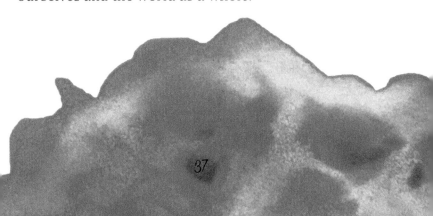

Step Three

~BUILDING SELF-LOVE

You Can Never Cross The Ocean,
Unless You Have
The Courage
To Lose Sight Of
The Shore.

-Christopher Columbus

A Positive Dialogue

Imagine you had a friend who followed you around, all day, every day, and spoke out loud to you the way you speak to yourself in your own mind. How long do you suppose you would allow that friendship to last?

It's often that most brutal of attacks -*comparison*- that leads the way in our assassinating our own character, and validating that we are indeed useless, unworthy, or even unlovable, all of which couldn't be further from the REAL truth, the real miracle of us.

Of course, these attacks are always going to be the result of such negative thinking.

To quote Albert Einstein:
"Everybody is a genius, but if you judge a fish by its ability to climb trees, it will live its life believing it's stupid."

You are unique. There is no one on this planet like you. Nobody has been born with your set of skills and abilities or personality in the way those things appear in you. This universe doesn't make mistakes; your creation serves a purpose—you have a purpose. You have been perfectly created to fill that purpose. Your skills, personality traits, and everything else that went into making you **you**, fits that purpose so perfectly that nobody else on this planet could do it as well as you. The world needs YOU just as you are.

You are a gift. However, most people don't even open the packaging; they are too busy comparing their wrapping

"EVERYBODY IS A
GENIUS. BUT IF YOU
JUDGE A FISH BY ITS
ABILITY TO CLIMB A
TREE, IT WILL LIVE ITS
WHOLE LIFE BELIEVING
THAT IT IS STUPID."

- ALBERT EINSTEIN

to other people's gifts. Stop comparing yourself to others; they are just as unique as you are.

It's like comparing a car to a horse, or a house to a tent. Those are things that perform similar functions, but are more perfect for different circumstances. Instead of comparing yourself, celebrate your uniqueness! So what if you can't do this or that? Focus on what you *can* do, because I promise you, that somewhere in all that, you will find your purpose and your inner joy.

Know that there is a purpose for each of us. So many of us go through life fixed and focused on our *'cant's'*, and on how others appear to be better than we are. So the tragedy is: We miss our own purpose. We go through life thinking we are useless, flightless fish that can't climb trees, when there are entire oceans out there just waiting for us. Instead of going swimming where we belong, we've been busy checking out the birds flitting effortlessly from tree to tree, and feeling inadequate.

If you have ever compared yourself, make today the day you stop. Give yourself the gift of self-acceptance. So what if there's a bunch of things you are not very good at? I can guarantee you that the things you're not that good at will have nothing to do with your life purpose. If there are people out there who are marvellous at the things that you're not, be happy for them, because it has something to do with their life purpose. There will be a whole new set of things, things you may not even have discovered yet, that will have everything to do with your life purpose; focus on that.

By being yourself you put something wonderful in the world that was not there before!

-Edwin Elliot

You will know when you find what is meant for you, because it will light you up. Seconds will slip into minutes, and minutes into hours, without your noticing. There will be a feeling of joy. That's your soul. That's how you speak its language—it lights you up.

Despite the fact that we have become proficient at lying to ourselves, there's an easy way to tell if something is for us or not. Our soul either becomes expanded or contracted when we encounter different things in life. What expands you also lights you up, fires you up, and gets you excited—your soul is saying *yes*, you are in alignment with who you truly are. Contraction, on the other hand, dulls your energy, kills your sparkle, and makes you curl almost completely in on yourself. It connects you to the void—this is the soul saying no.

If you are still having trouble seeing whether something is for you or not here's a great tip from the fabulous Marie Forleo; ask a good friend to watch you talk about whatever it is you're struggling with. If they know you well, they should be able to tell, just by looking at you, whether something expands or contracts you. They will see you either light up or go dull. Do what expands you. Say *NO* to what contracts you.

Finally, if whatever you're unsure of involves an income, ask yourself this: If I wasn't getting paid, but instead I could live on thin air, would I still want to do this? If you answered yes, it's in alignment with happiness, your soul, and the truth of you. If you say no, you have your answer—it's that simple.

"When I fully accept myself
I am freed from the burden of
needing outside acceptance"

- Joanna Hunter

Liar, Liar, Pants on Fire

Often we extend love and compassion to others that we wouldn't to ourselves. This is especially true if you are a parent, as well. How often have you given to others and sacrificed for yourself? How often have you said yes, when inside you're groaning and wishing you had the strength to say no?

This comes about because of bad habits we have picked up—it's learnt behaviour. Ultimately, it all spells out that more SELF-LOVE is needed. By the very action of saying yes, when we mean no, we are also lying, and we are limiting the energy that can flow to us by contracting our energy. The very word 'sacrifice' implies scarcity—not enough to go around—and if we are thinking it, we will be attracting it. By not honouring our own need to say no, we are informing the universe that we aren't worthy of what we need or want, and that we are not deserving of being taken care of. We are, in effect, punishing ourselves.

Since we set the standards by which the universe and others treat us, this becomes the standard by which our life treats us as well. Only we can change it.

**"You, Yourself, as much as anybody in the entire Universe,
Deserves your love and affection." ~ Buddha**

47

"You yourself, as much
as anybody in the entire
Universe, deserves your
love & affection"

- Buddha

I know of many people who seem to give and give. They give of their time, they give of their resources, and they give of their money and energy. They even seem to give the shirts off of their very backs. They are so generous that the universe should be showering them with everything their hearts desire. After all, *like energy attracts like energy*, so with all that giving, it should be returning back to them. It should be like *freaking* Christmas every day for them.

But it isn't because the universe gives back to us with the energy we are operating from. If we give from a place of lack, scarcity, and sacrifice, we will only ever receive lack, scarcity, and sacrifice in return—what I call a state of **"lack of"**. I use the term *"lack of"* to describe a state of energy from which you can only create more lack.

Think of your energy in terms of water. When you are aligned with yourself and your purpose, saying yes because you mean yes, your energy is crystal clear, like clean water. When you are doing something in an unaligned way, with tiredness, doubts, or resentment, saying yes when you should say no, your energy is cloudy and muddy, like dirty water.

We would never hand someone a glass of dirty water and expect them to drink it. However, that is what we are doing every time we take on tasks we really don't want to be a part of. When our own energy is not all it can be in that moment, saying "no" is as much an act of love for others as it is an act of self-love for ourselves.

Be Careful How You
Talk to Yourself Because
You are Listening!

-Lisa M. Hayes

A lot of us have forgotten that our primary relationship in life is with ourselves. From there, all other relationships flow. More importantly, by only saying yes when we mean it, we stop the lying to ourselves.

You will find it will become easier to respect yourself if you're not telling those big white lies. Set a higher standard. Begin that honest and open relationship with yourself.
Ask yourself this, and answer as honestly as you can (this is only between you and this page):

Do you really believe liars deserve all good things?

There is no right or wrong answer here....except when the answer does us no favours at all...

If you answered "no", that liars don't deserve all good things, yet you say "yes" all the time, when you *mean* "no", you are in big trouble. Why? Because saying something you don't really mean is lying, and in your own belief system, you don't believe liars deserve good things. This means that no good will come to you from the good you do, because it's coming from a dishonest place.

We need to stop being a liar; begin an honest and open relationship with yourself!

Many of us have lost sight of being true to ourselves. We're so busy trying to be good people to others, we've forgotten how to be good people to ourselves. That is the origin point of *"lack of"* within our own lives, the

" Your time is limited,
do not waste it living
someone else's life"

– Steve Jobs

original "scene of the crime" against ourselves. As with everything, this energy begins within us, and is then reflected back to us in our life experience. Therefore, it's paramount we try to change this energy at the core level.

Your own honesty and openness with yourself is like standing up for yourself. It has nothing to do with confrontation, or getting in anyone's face. It's an act of personal power and self-love to say no to an outside source, when in doing so, you say yes to yourself. You are saying, "I choose myself, I am worthy, and I am enough."

There is always going to be a few exceptions to every rule; let common sense prevail—I am not advocating that you leave new born babies to change their own diapers just because you are not feeling it today!

Start to listen to your feelings and respond to that input. By doing this, you are listening to and respecting yourself. As a side effect, you will be cleaning up your own energy vibration too. When I began living like this, my life began to blossom.

WE ONLY ACCEPT
THE LOVE WE THINK
WE DESERVE

-STEPHEN CHBOSKY

Liar Ping-Pong

Liar ping-pong works like this:

You may not have very high self-worth and you may not love yourself very much. Someone comes along and tells you that you are wonderful and that they love you. You really don't know where to put this; it's not how you feel about yourself. The bottom line is you really can't understand it! So, on a subconscious level, that person becomes a liar to you, and thus begins the game of 'liar ping-pong', as you bat their statement back to them. They will try and convince you that you are as wonderful as they think, but even if you want love, desperately seek it, you will be unable to accept it until you are willing to give love to yourself. We only get the love in life that we allow ourselves to have. It's up to us to allow ourselves all we need—hence the need to *Get Selfish*.

We become more loveable to ourselves by being true to ourselves, by accepting ourselves as we are, and by letting go of that most brutal of attacks on oneself: Comparison. Consciously accepting compliments with an open and grateful heart is a fantastic start to self-acceptance, but most of us find this very hard to do.

Often we bat compliments back just by habit. For example, someone says to us, "I love that top you have on." And we say, "Oh this old thing? It's nothing special." It's out of our mouths before we've even given it much thought.

To love
Oneself is
the beginning
of a life-long
Romance...

~Oscar Wilde

From this point onward, make a commitment to yourself to accept any and all compliments you get, with an open and grateful heart. Take a breath, smile, and just say, "*thank you*", as sincerely as you can. Accept the compliments, and take them into yourself; by doing so, you are putting yourself more in alignment with someone who deserves all good things. Of course, you will also be in the alignment of self-love.

Then breathe—which you'll really need to do if you've been on that Liar ping-pong leader board for a while, like I was. It gets easier, and eventually, saying thank you with a genuine smile becomes second nature, and it's just yummy when you believe it too.

Peace

Step Four

~BECOMING SELF-AWARE

When there are no enemies
within,
the enemies outside cannot
hurt you!

~ African proverb

Green Skin & Purple Hair

If I said to you, "You have green skin and purple hair," you wouldn't feel the need to rush to an actual mirror, or really react much at all. You would just **know** it isn't true and you would shrug it off, maybe even laugh at how stupid you feel that statement is. Water off a duck's back, right?

But, if you were not happy with your weight and someone said your dress made you look fat, it could be devastating.

We only react because a fear inside of ourselves is given a mirror, and we don't like what we see. An opportunity to heal if ever I saw one! The reactions we have are opportunities to heal our 'lacks'—nothing more. It's the universe's way of helping us, by highlighting an area where more love could live within us.

If we can heal ourselves of the self judgments that cause our insecurities, we will never be bothered by the judgements of others, or feel insecure by what others have said, again. Insecurity always stems from issues within us; negative beliefs that have been given energy, thus life. These issues may have started in our childhood or outside environment, but we have the power to dis-empower them by changing the way we think. And only *we* can do this for ourselves, because no one else can think or feel for us.

As human beings, we spend billions of dollars each year

You cannot control
the wind, but you
can direct the sail

-Proverb

filling the void our insecurities have created within us— if I could only be thinner, I would be okay! If I buy this stuff, it will all be better! If I impress these people, I will be likeable! If I do this, buy that, stand on my head, jump through these hoops, I can show everyone how great I am! Lack of self-love is what it really is, as well as lack of self-acceptance. Or, in terms of energy connecting to lack, the void of the place where love should live, instead of love itself.

You'll always be playing 'liar ping-pong' until you believe positive statements about yourself, and it's much easier to believe positive statements about yourself if you're not lying to yourself on a regular basis.

As a former world champ of 'liar ping-pong', I can tell you how freeing it is to put down your paddle, to know your own inner goodness, and feel truly, finally good enough. To know your own love, finally accepting yourself as you are, is the beginning of all good things.

"Since everything is a reflection of our minds... everything can be changed by our minds." ~Buddha

"Whatever we put our attention on will grow stronger in our life"

-Maharishi Mahesh Yogi

Filtered Perception

Our brains are these amazing super computers that are subject to what I call 'filtered perception'. We all have unconscious 'filters' in our consciousness, which actually organise and choose what we experience in our lives. Whatever we give our attention to expands, and we get more of it. Below is a great example of how it works...

Your friend buys a new car—you are a good friend, so you 'ooh and aah', and share your friend's new car excitement. You sniff the new car smell, you sit in it, stroke it, and talk about it. Nobody has a car like this— make, model, or even colour.

A couple of days later, you are driving along and you pass not one, but *three* cars of the same make, model, and even colour of your friend's car, and what's more, none of them are being driven by your friend.

What is going on? You could swear blind that you had never seen that make or model before!

Our brains are amazing; they are constantly recording and absorbing all of the information we encounter, which goes straight to our subconscious. Whatever ends up in our conscious brain, the part we are aware of, has to come through a filter; otherwise, we would be stuck on information overload. The thoughts we give our attention to determine what the filter is set for.

Since Everything is
a reflection of our
minds... ...Everything
Can be changed
by our Minds

~Buddha

Did everybody in the surrounding area lift their phones and say, "Hey, let's all get the same car?" Of course not! But by giving so much focus, energy, and attention to your friend's car, your amazing brain flipped a switch in your filter and began filtering *in* that type of car. They were always there, but since your brain deemed them unimportant (because before, you had never shown any attention or interest in them), it simply filtered them out.

Our beliefs create our actions and our actions create our results. That's fantastic if you have positive happy beliefs, but not so great if you have self-limiting beliefs.

Self-limiting beliefs do exactly what they say on the tin: They limit us, or—as I like to think of them—they limit the energy that can be exchanged or flow to us.

Beliefs flip the switches on our filters—some cause things to be filtered in and others to be filtered out. Our own unique beliefs create a filter, which we then see the world through. It literally creates your reality. What's more, our filters pattern-match and give you evidence to back them up. They do this by deleting and distorting anything that doesn't match the information that is flowing to you. They create a type of distorted reality for you.

This is one of the reasons why police officers sometimes have such a hard time taking statements from multiple witnesses. We view the world not as *it* is, but as *we are*. Our filters are working away whether we are aware of them or not. This is how we see life.

"WE DON'T SEE THINGS
AS THEY ARE, WE SEE
THEM AS WE ARE."

- ANAÏS NIN

Have you ever heard the term "rose-tinted glasses"? It works just like that. Those rose tinted glasses make everything look rosy. Your filters will make everything look like whatever the filter is set to.

Bet you can guess how I perceived life when I held the belief that "life is shit". Ye-ah, it wasn't pretty!

F-E-A-R HAS TWO MEANINGS:

FORGET EVERYTHING AND RUN
OR
FACE EVERYTHING AND RISE

-THE CHOICE IS YOURS

~ZIG ZIGLAR

The Mirrors of Our Fears

FEAR is what keeps us weak, small, stuck, disconnected from all good, and ultimately leaves us in a cycle of feeling bad. It is created by the void where love should live, thus its nature is lack. It exists at that point where we disconnect from the truth of who we are—our soul.

Any and all reactions that do not feel good stem from fear. Fear is an illusion, another lie we tell ourselves. So, if something causes you to react negatively, know it is fear. You must look inside yourself to find the root cause. What part of you is scared?

For example, we see a beautiful woman driving a sports car with the top down and her designer shades on. Our immediate reaction may be: BITCH!

Now, we don't know this woman—she could be Mother Teresa incarnate for all we know—but the reaction popped into our heads none the less, as if by magic. Where did it come from? If we have chosen to take personal responsibility for our thoughts we'll know it was all us. But where inside us is feeling like this?

Our outside world is like a mirror to our inner one. That outside mirror is constantly giving us opportunities to heal the inner world; to fix our 'filters'. Remember, the outside world was attracted in through the vibration of our thoughts—the energy from which we are operating, either the abundant source or the lack-filled void.

A loving person
lives in a loving
world. A hostile
person lives in a
hostile world.
Everyone you meet
is your mirror.

– Ken Keyes Jr

There are different mirrors. In understanding these, we are well on our way to transforming our fear into love. When we do this, we become spiritual alchemists. Here are the mirrors we face:

Mirror of Desire: *We want what she has.* We want to be driving that sports car without a care in the world, wearing expensive designer shades—that is the Mirror of Desire. So we voice the fears around our not having those things—I am not good enough for those things, or I may never have those things, or there aren't enough of those things to go around—because we are in "lack" consciousness. Why should she have them? And so our response is, "BITCH".

Mirror of Self: *We see ourselves in her.* We have the sports car and the ridiculously expensive shades, and we don't like that behaviour in ourselves, so we give a voice to that fear: BITCH! What we are really saying is *I am a bitch, I don't like myself. I don't feel good enough despite the pretty things I have.* Those thoughts stem from the kind relationship we are having with ourselves. A call to learn to love oneself - nothing less will heal it.

Mirror of Avoidance: *I will never be like that!* When we have an aversion to something, it reflects a tendency towards the very thing we avoid. For example, we don't have or want the sports car, but we are uncomfortable with the behaviour of the lady, because we see it, let's say, as a need for one-up-man-ship. We see it this way, because deep inside we have the same need, which we may, or may not, be able to express. And instead of recognising that the need for one-up-man-ship stems

"WHATEVER IS REJECTED
FROM THE SELF,
APPEARS IN THE WORLD
AS AN EVENT."

- CARL JUNG

from a fear of not being good enough, we give a voice to our fear: BITCH! Once more, the need for one-up-man-ship is simply a cry for more self-love.

Mirror of Memory: *Conditioning*. We have the memory of another woman who drove a sports car, someone we didn't like, or who might have hurt us once. So basically, you have nothing against the actual woman driving the sports car, but subconsciously, or even consciously, our mind 'pattern-matched,' connecting this woman to the one we have bad feelings about. Fears from your past give voice to what seems like a fear in the present and... *voilà*: BITCH! This fear comes from the fear that the person who hurt us might have been right, or in other words: Self-doubt.

The truth is: You are an unlimited being of pure *source* energy, expressing itself in a human body. You are magnificent! The source, of who you are, created all that you see. How could you be anything else but brilliant and worthy? The good news is: These are all opportunities to heal, and to bring ourselves back to a place of non-reaction. These are opportunities to re-connect with our own *SOULS*, and our own fountains of *INNER PEACE*. Each of these mirrors are healed in the same way: Through *SELF-LOVE*.

And self-love starts by being true to yourself.

First of all, we need an open, honest, and frank dialogue with ourselves. We need to give ourselves that which is missing inside of us.
We need to **Get Selfish. The way is through!**

YOU Rock! Think about it- you have gotten to this age & you're still here! That means you have a 100% track record for getting through life!

– Joanna Hunter

The Way is Through

We don't get what we want by going around it—avoidance doesn't get to the heart of any experience, nor make it go away. It only limits our experience of life and our personal growth. Life, and its many experiences, is something we all have to go *through*! There is no other way!

Grief is a good example. None of us want to experience it, but it's inevitable, and once it hits us, it's unavoidable. We can't get around grief, we have to go through it to get out the other side. We need to go through those five stages that the experts have defined in order to come to terms with our loss and learn to live constructively with it. If we allow ourselves to go through grief, we can gain greater understanding and compassion, for ourselves and others, and become more appreciative of what we have in the present. If we try to avoid grief (which is ultimately impossible), we end up shutting down parts of ourselves, and stopping the flow of happiness and abundance in our lives. We cannot selectively numb.

Going through has three key elements:

The first element is: *There has to be a willingness to face the behaviour or issue we want to change.*

All change requires an element of courage; however, this can sometimes be hard to come by, especially if the behaviour has been going on a while. I am often heard saying, "I like it when my life coaching clients are pissed off." Not with me, of course, and it's not because I am a

The quickest way to acquire
Self-Confidence is to do
exactly what you are afraid
to do.

- Anon

sadist or a big meanie, but because anger is a kind of Dutch courage.

Have you ever become so angry that you have gone from a wishy-washy feeling of something-needs-to-change-but-I'm-waiting-on-the-knight-in-shining-armour! to a super assertive; hell-hounds-won't-stop-me-this-WILL-change-and-I-will-be-the-one-to-change-it?   Change is actually a space where anger can be a useful emotion - a great motivator to bringing you *through*.   It's my experience that being angry demands action, and change inevitably follows. However, courage and willingness to change, if you have them, are a much less stressful way. Either way, become committed to change, it starts with a willingness to **want** to change.

The second element is: *Gaining the knowledge of how to change!*

The sad reality is that most people's **'can'ts'** are really just unmet educational needs, obscuring the practical **'hows',** which they can never get to, because of their attachment to the **'can'ts'.**

We often say "*oh that can't happen*", or "*that won't happen*", or my personal favourite: "*That will **never** happen!*" Such a strong statement! It might sound harsh, but I have a saying—and if you're a student of mine, you will know it well—"Can or can't, either way you are right!" We are all creating our own reality with our own thoughts, and I can't help anyone if, to begin with, they don't even believe the solution exists. They won't be able to see it even if I show it to them.

Believe You Can
-&-
You're Halfway There.

-Theodore Roosevelt

Our beliefs create our filters, and our filters will back up our beliefs.

Your beliefs have a direct effect on your results.

Yes, your beliefs are that powerful!

So, before we use strong negative statements, such as **'can't', 'won't',** and **'never',** which shape our beliefs, thus our results, we need to check that we are **not**, in fact, substituting those words for **'I don't know how'**. Saying and thinking 'I don't know how' is not the same, energetically, as saying or thinking **'can't', 'won't',** and **'never'**. I don't know is simply an admission of a lack of knowledge and nothing more. By admitting that we *don't know how*, we open our energy up to the solution, instead of closing ourselves off from it with **'can't'**. Saying we **'don't know how'**, rather than **'can't'**, invites the possibility of learning into our lives, and we change our situation from something impossible to change, to something we just haven't figured out how to change **yet**. Everything can be figured out!

The third element is: *Acceptance.*

To bring more happiness and abundance into our lives, we need to make friends with who we are, and accept the warts-and-all versions of ourselves and the situations in our lives. We need to love ourselves in all the places and for all the things that we find hard to love, just as they are. This is our truth, and it reconnects us to our *'source'*, and to all the good stuff the universe has to offer.

Happiness Can Exist
Only In Acceptance

- George Orwell

Reconnecting to our truth is what creates that greater connection to the abundant source energy within the universe, which is also the core of us—our soul.

If we want happiness and abundance—*the way is through* the very things that prevent it from being in our lives: Our own *'lack'* of consciousness. We also need to accept situations for what they are, too, before they can be healed. We need to first go through our lack in order to fill ourselves up.

This is why it's so important to **Get Selfish**!

Laughter

Step Five

~ALIGNMENT TO HAPPY

You Reap What You Sow

~Proverb

Alignment

What do you want in life? What would fill you up? What in life would bring you the greatest joy?

Those are big questions—ones that I spent a really long time (some would say way too much time) pondering. Then I had a moment of inspiration: If I simply asked the universe for happiness, happiness would fill me up, and bring me the greatest joy. Surely happiness was what I was really seeking. I figured that I couldn't be happy and have a terrible life at the same time! It had to be a one-or-the-other thing!

However, with my 'inspiration' came the realisation that I really didn't know very much about my happiness, or happiness in general.

What I *did* know was unhappiness. I had become somewhat of an expert in that field. I knew that chasing and attaching value to material things didn't produce lasting happiness—seriously, I owned several designer handbags that attest to that fact. A designer handbag could give me fleeting happiness, but not that spiritual kind that makes people glow from the inside. Till this point, I had only managed to create the kind of happiness that fades: *Designer-bag-happiness.* What I wanted was *Dalai-Lama-happiness.*

I needed to stop attaching material things to the idea of happiness, and accept that happiness is not based on material things, but on feelings.

"*Human Happiness &
Human Satisfaction
Must Ultimately Come
From Within Oneself*"

-Dalai Lama

I began to see that to have happiness, I needed to align myself with the vibration of it. In order to feel good, we have to take ourselves to that place.

Happiness can't happen if you stay *stuck* in thoughts, feelings, and situations that serve unhappiness.

This meant that behaviours, attitudes, and thoughts that didn't serve happiness needed to go from my life, as well as people, places, situations, and anything else that did not align with or serve happiness.

Yes, this was a scary step! But what was more frightening in my mind was the thought of years more of unhappiness, when the solution to my happiness was right there. In the long run, moving away from things that make you unhappy must serve that which makes you happy—it's simple logic.

Yet again there is a choice: You either make peace with the things that make you unhappy, or you simply move your energy away from the unhappiness, and move towards things that light you up and make you feel good.

Your alignment is really important, because your thoughts create your beliefs, your beliefs create your actions, and your actions create your results, which just reaffirm your beliefs, since they set the filters which determine how you experience and view life... and round we go again. It's like that lone suitcase on the baggage reclaim.

LIVE YOUR BELIEFS
AND YOU CAN TURN
THE WORLD
AROUND.

-HENRY DAVID THOREAU

Our energy vibrations are created by our thoughts, beliefs, and feelings, and they attract life experience that carries the same energy vibrations. Thus, our reality is created by what we are putting out. The universe is mirroring back to you your predominant energy. So, isn't it time you aligned with something better?

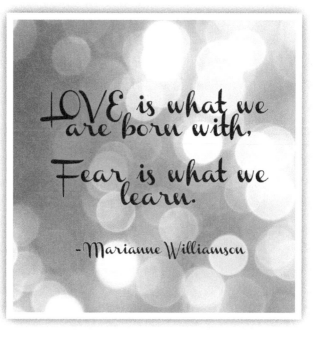

LOVE is what we are born with.

Fear is what we learn.

-Marianne Williamson

Love & Fear

Love is the one true emotional state in the entire universe. However, on earth we divide it into two feelings, two seemingly opposing emotions: Love and fear. Love is a state of abundance and the source of everything, while fear is simply a lack of love, which creates a void where love should live. Every emotion that has ever been felt can be boiled down to one of these two perceived emotional states, and one or the other of these *'Power House Emotions'* is always in operation within our reality.

Love and fear are also the gatekeepers of the **'winner'** and **'victim'** mentalities.

It is easy to tell which one of these emotions is in operation at any one time. Anything that makes us feel bad, makes us feel unworthy—be it guilt, hopelessness, anger, frustration, annoyance, depression, hate, helplessness, darkness, shame or negativity—boils down to fear, and a simple lack of love. This connects our soul to a void, or the *victim* in us, and feelings of lack.

On the bright side, anything that makes us feel good: Happiness, joy, peace, gratitude, feelings of ease, abundance, lightness, warmth, the feelings that make us smile and lift us up, all of that good stuff boils down to **love**. This connects our soul to the light, which is also the nature of our soul—that abundant *winner*—therefore abundance and happiness have to flow.

Love Liberates

-Maya Angelou

By asking ourselves "how we feel" in any given moment, we can instantly see what we are aligned to. If we feel good, we are aligned to the powerhouse of love. In that reality, all good things exist and are possible; it is an infinitely abundant and connected reality. When we feel good, we are aligned to and tapping into that reality. Here, all things are possible, and we may create the life we wish—we *'win'* at life.

However, if we feel bad we are aligned to the powerhouse emotion of *fear*. We are limited; there is a feeling that all bad things are waiting to get us. We feel a great sense of lack, and we are disconnected from our source. Here we are kept small and in the cycle of being a victim.

The good news is we have free will. We can choose which reality we want to inhabit by changing our thoughts. As feelings are a by-product of our thoughts, we can continuously monitor our alignment without having to monitor the 60,000 or so thoughts we experience each and every day.

We need to be mindful to monitor and adjust our alignment to fit our goals. If we want happiness, for example, we need to remove what makes us unhappy from our lives and do things that we know make us happy. But, we also need to think long-term with each of our actions. For example, a bar of chocolate might make you temporarily happy, but is it ultimately nurturing for your body, that glorious home for your soul? And if you feel guilty eating it, is it serving your inner *winner* or your inner *victim*?

Joy

Step Six

~BECOMING EMPOWERED

Respect Yourself enough
to walk away from anything
that no longer serves you,
grows you or makes you
happy!

-Anon

Personal Responsibility

Personal responsibility is another term for 'how to empower yourself'. That's what personal responsibility really is: The key to unlocking your empowerment and stepping out as a *'winner'* in life, instead of a *'victim'.* The difference between being a winner or a victim is not about the outer circumstances of their lives, but about their inner choices. A winner is someone who takes personal responsibility for their life and their own thoughts and feelings. They feel empowered to take whatever inner or outer action is necessary to make the best of their life. A victim is dis-empowered by the belief that they are helpless in the face of circumstances, people, and feelings beyond their control.

Empowerment cannot be given or taken away by another. It can only be bestowed upon your 'self', by your 'self'. It is a choice, an empowered mindset.

The problem here, though, is that many see empowerment as something outside of themselves. I believe my clients when they tell me they have no problem with empowerment; however, my definition of the word has become all-encompassing, and theirs might not be, therefore creating the paradox I call, *'the part-time victim'*.

Many of my clients tell me they have no problem with empowering themselves; they take charge and they mean it. I am sure they do; however as in the next breath, they will tell me how so-and-so **makes** them feel so angry, or

I believe there is an
inner power that
makes Winners or
Losers.
And the winners are
those who really listen
to the truth of their
HEART.

- Sylvester Stallone

makes them do something they'd rather not be part of. "How does that *really* work?" I ask them. "How many people have you got in that brain of yours? Who's actually doing the thinking and reacting for you? Surely if others can MAKE YOU feel... XY or Z... then it's not just you in that brain of yours choosing to think those thoughts that make you miserable?"

True empowerment is taking total responsibility, for all of me. It's taking responsibility for all my thoughts, all my feelings (which are by-products of those thoughts), all my actions, all my deeds, all of my spoken words, all of my energy—not just part of my energy:

ALL OF MY ENERGY!

The following *feelings* are all signs that you've taken a detour and have dis-empowered yourself by choosing a way of thinking that leads to a 'victim' mentality, instead of a 'winner' mindset.

The great news is that you can choose to change any of the *thoughts* that put you in the victim role and switch instead to the kind of thinking that will allow you to be the winner we all deserve to be.

Lack	Impatience	Blame
Upset	Fatigue	Depression
Anger	Vengeance	Complaining
Helplessness	Self-pity	Jealousy

"The Primary Cause for
unhappiness
is never the situation
but your thoughts
about it"

-Eckhart Tolle

Remember, all the universe is energy, and so are these emotional states—they are pure energy. The feelings in the table above are what I call 'closed' or 'contracted'. They close off the amount of energy that can be exchanged between us and the world, limiting and blocking the flow of good things, to and from us. They all have one thing in common: None of these will ever feel good in the long run. The bad feelings we get are our soul's way of warning us that we are contracting, drawing in, connecting to the void, instead of the source of all abundance.

If you are not feeling good, I can promise you that you are operating from an unempowered mentality. The empowered mentality opens up our energy, allowing an unlimited amount of energy to flow to us, and it always feels good. If you recognise in yourself any of the feelings from the table above, don't worry; your thoughts just need a little adjustment to get you back to the winning/empowered state and on your journey.

The table below shows some of the empowered states of being. They all have one thing in common: They make you feel good because they connect you to your soul—the source of all happiness and abundance.

Joy	Patience	Ownership
Peace	Sharing	Ease
Abundance	Forgiveness	Love
Happiness	Creative Flow	Gratitude

I Know For Sure That What we Dwell on is Who we Become

-Oprah Winfrey

If you want to go places in your life, make today the day you choose not to let anyone else ever **make** you feel anything ever again, without your express permission. There is no power in disempowered energy or thinking. It just creates more helplessness, more sick and tired of being sick and tired, more of the need to complain, more of the victim whose life is miserable! If you don't want to be in that place, make a commitment to yourself to change the thoughts that created it. Hit the emergency brake on your excuses, on why you can't show up larger in your own life.

Ultimately, whether you believe this or not, it's your choice what to think, and therefore how to feel. That's why empowerment has to start inside your own head. When you find yourself in a pity party for one, it's up to you to empower yourself to end it. Just admitting this type of behaviour will not solve the problem. Loving yourself enough to take ownership and find a solution is the way. If you let yourself slip into that victim mode, where life is kicking your ass and there's nothing you can do about it, that's all you'll get, because that'll be the energy place inside you, from which you will be drawing all your experiences from.

Choosing to empower yourself by putting a stop to the pity party—that's the place where everything you've ever wanted to be in your human experience lives! By stepping into your power, through shifting your thoughts, all becomes possible. It's about taking personal responsibility and recognising that the bad stuff is just fear, and knowing it is **you** that ultimately empowers **your** fear.

"I DO NOT FIX MY PROBLEMS.
I FIX MY THINKING.
THEN MY PROBLEMS FIX
THEMSELVES."

-LOUISE HAY

You can just as easily unempower it by making a different choice. The pay-off for choosing to empower yourself is HUGE - it is emotional control of your life. It is what will create a beautiful journey, instead of a crazy, strapped-in horror-ride you can do nothing about.

Shallow men believe in luck and circumstance. Strong men believe in cause and effect

~Ralph Waldo Emerson

The Pay-Off

I want to highlight the energy of what I call, "The Pay-Off". You see, we often associate a pay-off with something good, like a reward. Rewards are positive, right? Here's the truth, not always. Not understanding this can be that burst tire on the way to the airport and you are going nowhere!

Everything we tend to do as human beings has a kind of pay-off. We can't shift a type of behaviour until we are aware of it. This is why I also want to highlight the negative aspects of the pay-off.

Victim behaviours have massive pay-offs. When you are the victim of your life, the pay-off is: It's not your fault! You have no control and no say—trust me, this is a pay-off! It means every time you perceive something as going wrong in your life, you can off-load any responsibility for whatever happened, and it's a wallow-at-your-hearts-content pass—a bit like a get-out-of-jail-free card. It's not your fault! You had no control! NO CHOICE! A lovely pay-off! Unfortunately, it also takes your power in life with it.

You see, there's always a choice. People may do many things to us, but our minds will always remain our own. That is the true nature of free will; your ability to choose one thought over another. So, despite what went on, you can still choose. You might not be able to choose the circumstances, but we can always choose how to perceive and feel about them.

You've got to kick fear to the side, because the payoff is **HUGE.**

-Mariska Hargitay

Our own pay-offs are often what keep us stuck and repeating old patterns. If you can see where your own behaviour has been more in alignment with victim behaviour, ask yourself what your pay-off is for staying stuck. Is it a fear that you have not acknowledged? As soon as we become aware of something, we can change it. By changing our thoughts, deeds, and actions, therefore changing our alignment, we change our vibration and frequency, and we **will** attract in a different result. It can be no other way. This is actually physics.

Step Seven

~PUTTING IT ALL TOGETHER

The Law of Manifestation

The Law of Manifestation simply states:

"Like energy attracts like energy."

Let's really look at this statement. Albert Einstein, one of the greatest thinkers of the twentieth century, surmised that in this universe 'everything is energy!' EVERYTHING! That makes our statement *'Like energy attracts like energy'* **huge**! That means that if everything is energy, everything in the entire universe can be attracted or repelled. That 'everything' includes *your* happiness, joy, fulfilment, and abundance in life.

We humans are capable of **Conscious Thought**. In other words, we can choose what thoughts to think. We have conscious awareness. Here's where it gets really interesting...

Your thoughts can be measured. They have an electrical output, an energy, and therefore a frequency and a vibration. They are an actual force within this universe. So, this is the point when this stuff really gets REAL... **Like energy attracts Like energy**—your thoughts are pure energy—you can choose your thoughts—which by their very nature must attract like energy to them— since everything is energy—**your thoughts can attract and repel EVERYTHING!**

Just take a few minutes to ponder this information.

When your desires
    are strong enough,
You will appear to
    possess Superhuman
powers to
    Achieve!

-Napoleon Hill

If its new to you, re-read it, by all means—let this information really sink in, because this is massive and the keys to your happy, fulfilled, abundant life.

It's important that you understand it. Your life experience is attracted in by your thoughts. What you give the most energy to must show up in your life.

To fully sum up, the genius that was Albert Einstein, again, said it best:

"Everything is energy and that is all there is to it. Match the frequency of the reality you want and you will get that reality. There can be no other way. This is not philosophy. This is physics."

It's one of my favourite quotes. It shows Einstein's understanding of both physics and of the Law of Manifestation. More importantly, it bases the Law of Manifestation on scientific fact. Back when I was still very much searching for happiness, it meant a lot to me that the Law of Manifestation was based on hard science. It was measurable; results could be duplicated over and over again. I needed that.

It meant my happiness was not a planet-aligning-once-in-a-blue-moon-stand-on-your-head-and-chant-a-funky-mantra thing. It meant if I applied the principles of the Law of Manifestation to my life, I would get quantifiable, consistent results, and you can too!

If you want to find the secrets of the universe, think in terms of energy, frequency and vibration

~Nikola Tesla

The Manifestation Process

Creating anything you want or desire in life is easy. It follows only three steps:

Asking, Knowing, and Receiving

1. ASKING

Put it out there; speak it out loud, write it down, ask God, the universe, your angels, Tom Cruise, Gandhi—it doesn't matter how you do it, just that you are very CLEAR about what you want. Speak like you already have it. Speaking like you already have it is very important, as the universe responds to your energy vibration.

For example, if you say, "*I am **getting** that car*", the universe will respond to **'getting'**. **Getting** is not ownership or possession of the thing you want. Using the thought **'getting',** which is a process, not a result, creates a frequency that will only ever attract the *action of getting*—which is not the same as *'having'.*

What I use is borrowed from the wonderful Bob Proctor: *"I am so blessed and grateful now that I have_____ (fill in the blank)"* As you can see, I am aligning with the energy of 'having' instead of 'getting' and it will attract 'having'.

The way we ask is quite important, because it creates the initial energy that all other energies will resonate with and become attracted too. It's like powering up the magnet.

TRUST IS THE FIRST STEP TO LOVE.

-MUNSHI PREMCHAND

2. KNOWING

You don't need to ask over and over for what you want, you only have to *believe*, to *know* you are going to receive. You have to let yourself be certain that it's going to be delivered, in the same way as when you ask a waiter for a dish, you **know** it will be delivered. And then you have to let it go. Letting go is one of the most important steps.

For example; you don't feel the need to follow that waiter into the kitchen and look over the chef's shoulder as he puts your meal together, then follow the waiter back to the table and watch him deliver said meal, do you? If you do, quit bugging the waiter! You'll get much better service trusting him! If you ask the universe for something over and over, you are also bugging the waiter, and tapping into the energy of your 'lack', rather than the certainty of 'having'. And guess what the universe is going to deliver? LACK!

TRUST the universe to get your order so right it will exceed your wildest imagination. What you've asked for has to become a 'knowing', a certainty within your belief system.

"When you are grateful,
   fear disappears and
      abundance appears."

-Anthony Robbins

3. RECEIVING

Any blocks to receiving do not come from an infinitely abundant universe. The clue is in the infinitely abundant part!

The blocks come from bugging the waiter, which boils down to your FEAR that you are not getting what you want—that there is a *'lack of',* or that you are not worthy of what you have asked for—the old fear of not being good enough.

Whatever reason you are not receiving, the cause is always FEAR. Nothing vanquishes fear like *love*. Look inside yourself and **LOVE**. Connect to your own source of abundance. That removes all the blocks, so that the only result can be delivery.

This knowledge of the Law of Manifestation process is enough to begin positive changes in your life on its own. However, the *'Get Selfish'* method to happiness and fulfilment will also help you to clean up your vibration! It all starts with listening to, loving, and accepting yourself. Even if you created your life by default, without conscious intention before, your new 'self-love' energy base will create you a great life, a life you'll love on every level. Once you love yourself, you will hold the universe in the palm of your hand. The universe has to respond with love. It can be no other way!

"MAY YOUR
CHOICE REFLECT
YOUR HOPES
NOT YOUR
FEARS."

-NELSON MANDELA

The Choice

Our daily choice:

Do you want to live in an infinitely abundant universe?

Or

Do you want to live in a universe of lack, where there is never going to be enough?

The choice is yours. When you choose, you need to make sure your words, actions, and deeds reflect that choice in order to bring it into your reality. Are your actions, thoughts, and deeds aligned to your success? Or are you contradicting your desire for success at every turn?

If, for example, you tell the universe you want to be successful, but every time you attempt to do something that puts you in alignment with that, you internally call yourself a loser, you are giving the universe a double message, and it will align itself to the one with the most energy. Since you don't really believe in yourself, the universe won't either.

This is why it's so important to make friends with yourself, to believe that you are enough, that you are worthy of all good things, because the universe will always reflect back to you, your predominant thoughts and feelings. Developing self-love and acceptance is cutting yourself a break.

Your Power is in your
Thoughts,
So stay awake,
In other words,
Remember to
REMEMBER!

~Rhoda Bryne

The choice is more than just choosing; you also need to be in alignment with it. This is what I believe Mahatma Gandhi meant by, *"Be the change you wish to see in the world."*

Be your own change. Become the change you desire and it's yours, there can be no other way.

You have created your current reality—whether you believe it or not, you are already an expert 'manifestor'. If you don't like the reality you've got, it certainly doesn't mean you **wanted** the bad stuff to happen—absolutely not! It just means you've been creating by default—that robotic state of being without conscious thought, intention and understanding. Perhaps you had a lot of fear, and worries, so much so they became your vibration, they would then attract in like experiences.

If you don't like the current reality you are experiencing, forgive yourself; don't make it another opportunity to bash yourself. Instead, love yourself. You were doing the best you could with the information you had. Build a bridge over self-pity-falls and move swiftly along. You have new information and you can do better now; it's just a choice away.

Now you might be thinking, 'it can't be that simple,' I can assure you, it is. I get up every morning and thank my lucky stars it works, that I have gone from being a passenger in my life to being the driver. I did it all with my thoughts, and you can too. The proof is in the pudding, so I invite you to pick up a spoon and dive right in!

ALWAYS REMEMBER
YOUR LIFE IS SERVING
YOU, EVERY SECOND OF
EVERY DAY, EVEN IF
YOU DON'T
UNDERSTAND HOW.

-JOANNA HUNTER

The Perfect Life

Your life is perfect—yes, really!

It is perfect in that it perfectly serves the spiritual evolution of your soul. There are no mistakes, everything in your life is unfolding as it's meant to be. Each trial or challenge you face is perfectly serving your immortal **soul's** purpose in that moment, thus teaching you something about yourself. You are perfect. Your unique skills and personality traits could not be more perfectly made for your life and for your life lessons.

That means right here, right now, is where you're meant to be! In this very moment, your life is serving you and giving you tailor-made opportunities to know who you really are. Opportunities to know your own goodness, your own strength, to find a fountain of inner peace so abundant you will never run out, to connect with the source of all light so bright, it will shine in every corner of your life and in the lives of those you encounter.

"Your Life is Perfect!" Ha! When I first heard this, it was given to me in a meditation by my guide. I was so annoyed that I didn't meditate for two whole months afterwards. At that time, my life was a million miles away from what I perceived as perfect. I was SO angry when I heard the words: Your life is perfect. I ranted, "How can all this BS be perfect?!"

I realise now that we are here to learn and to expand our immortal souls—amazing what happens when you go

IF YOU CHANGE THE WAY
YOU LOOK AT THINGS YOU
WILL CHANGE THE THINGS
YOU SEE!

-WAYNE DYER

back to meditation and, well... meditate on it. (Sheepish, who me?) When we understand that we are souls, who happen to have bodies, we can begin to appreciate how wonderful this place truly is, as a classroom for an immortal being. Nothing ever done to you or someone you love is permanent—your energy is immortal. This life time is but a blink of an eye.

Everything is teaching us and expanding us and there are no bad lessons! The lessons just *are.* This very moment in time is serving us on a higher level. All those things we might think are annoying or that we feel 'why me?' about, are serving us, even if we don't understand it in the present moment!

When faced with a challenge in my life, I now ask, "What is this teaching me?" Once you become aware of the lesson, the need for it disappears, along with the challenge that brought it.

As I look on my life, I can now appreciate things that almost broke me as I was going through them, and realize that they are also the greatest things to have happened to me. When I look in the mirror, I love the person I see, because I have fought hard to become her—and you know what? She's pretty awesome, and so are you!

Your life, however it looks, is serving your soul, preparing you for the next step. Knowing this, we can truly appreciate the truth of our lives, already being perfect, and just... RELAX!

If all you did was just
look for things to
appreciate you would
live a joyous, spectacular
life

-Abraham- Hicks

Gratitude

The simplest and easiest way to align yourself with the creative and connective power of the universe, and therefore your own soul, is to feel Gratitude.

Gratitude feels good and is firmly rooted in the powerhouse emotion of LOVE, and since **"like energy attracts like energy"**, love and gratitude are emotions we want to be aligned to, on a consistent basis. Gratitude is the super highway to feeling good.

Make it your mission to find things that make you grateful. Start by finding ten things each day to be grateful for, even if they seem really little, because this will powerfully draw in more things to be grateful for. The goal here is simply to feel **good**.

For example: I am grateful for my car, which takes me from A to B, or I am grateful that I have a roof over my head, or even I am grateful that I have eyes to read this. The list is endless. What's more, you can think of things to be grateful for anywhere—on public transport, in your car, shower, bath, while shopping, at work, at the gym, even your daily chores can be transformed with gratitude. Just thinking of what you are grateful for aligns your vibration to LOVE, and that in turn attracts in more things for you to love, including:

A life you will love.

Gratitude makes sense of our past, brings peace for today, and creates a vision for tomorrow.

~Melody Beattie

Just start to think of what you can put on your list. Make it a daily habit. Make it fun! How many did you find to be grateful for yesterday? Can you top it today?

However, the trick here is to **feel** the gratitude. It is not enough to just say it; there needs to be a feeling with it, to make sure it puts you on the vibration of gratitude and love. So, focus only on the things you're really grateful for, and let your heart open up. Feel the feelings of gratitude, (NO ifs or buts), just really *feel* the feelings, as these will bring more feel-good feelings forward.

If you are feeling it, you're thinking it, and if you're thinking it, you are attracting it!

If you have forgotten what a miracle looks like, get up right now, and turn the tap on! Running water. Now take just a moment to appreciate all that went into, that water coming out of your tap. The people, the designers, the worker, the ease by which you turned the tap on! Do you know where your nearest well is, with clean safe drinking water? Wouldn't it be a hassle to go fetch that every day? Bet that tap is looking more and more like a modern day miracle!

Include yourself in your gratitude, appreciate, praise and bless your awesome self. Share your gratitude; a little goes a long way. Show your gratitude to others; who doesn't like to be appreciated? Be a giver of gratitude daily, making it your way of life. You will be powerfully aligning your energy to all the good things you want to have in your life.

GRATITUDE– THE GAME CHANGER OF LIFE!

A journey of 1000 miles starts with a single step, so go easy on yourself. These little steps will come together to form a larger, much more positive picture for your soul's experience.

The universe rewards grateful people, by giving you more things to be grateful for.

If you just take away just one thing from this book—let it be that you adopt:

The attitude of gratitude, because it is the game-changer of life!

Acknowledgements

I have a list of people I would like to thank, people that have my sincere heartfelt gratitude for their help in the creation of this book. First, I want to thank the ever-present source of grace in my life that I call the universe, that for many years hinted and whispered a quiet song, always there just like a longing, until I began listening, respecting, and loving myself, and then its voice grew louder, clearer, and became my guides—a brilliant resource that speaks my language. In coming to know this energy, I am so grateful that I know now I am not separate from it, but a droplet of it—that we all are.

I want to thank all people who have inspired me, supported me, and believed in this little book that the universe co-wrote with me. So, in no particular order: My husband Paul Hunter, and my beautiful children, Daniel, Ellen, and Katie. My family, mother and brother, all my amazing friends that encouraged me on this journey, especially, Paulyne Brown and Liam Wood. Special thanks to Theresa MacGillivray and Anne-Marie Carlin for their hard work and insights. All the friends who have shown such enthusiasm for my book, and all my inspiring clients, who leave me in awe of their stories, their bravery and courage to change—that they dared to believe in better. You are my everyday sheroes and heroes. Finally, to you dear reader, my heartfelt gratitude.

THANK YOU!

BE THE CHANGE YOU WISH
TO SEE IN THE WORLD

-MAHATMA GHANDI

About Joanna Hunter

Born in Stockholm, Sweden, Joanna moved to the Highlands of Scotland at the tender age of nine, where her soul has found its calling in helping others as a Mama, Wife, and Intuitive Life and Business Coach.

Her experiences have taken her from the high-flying world of fashion, to running her own shops, and winning accolades in the business world, to dark nights of the Soul. On the way, she once more awakened her gift of mediumship by honouring her primary relationship with herself. Joanna has developed her passion for teaching, all things spiritual and beyond. Today she gives talks, lectures and workshops with the aid of her spirit team (the co-writers of this book), aptly named 'the transition team.' Together they help people transition from an asleep state of being to an awakened, empowered state of being.

For Joanna, being passionate about self-enrichment is not simply a choice, but a beautiful calling of her soul.

If you want to know more, Joanna can be found sharing wisdom, tips, and the light of her spiritual transition team at **www.facebook.com/joannahuntercom** or at **www.joannahunter.com**.

The website for this book is **www.getselfishbook.com**.

Please look out for future publications.

Notes

Notes

Lightning Source UK Ltd.
Milton Keynes UK
UKOW07f1039080715

254799UK00014B/32/P